peaceful
meditations

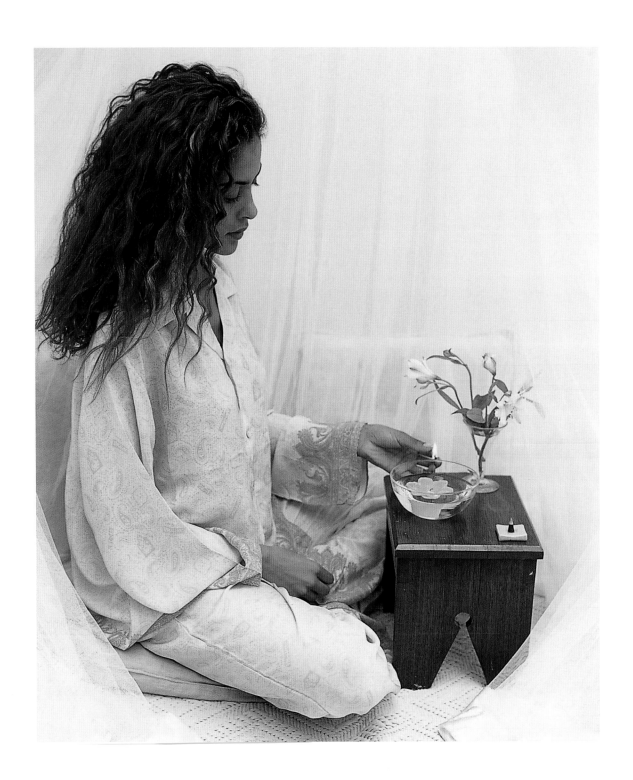

peaceful
meditations

focus the mind to achieve
peace and serenity

Tracey Kelly

LORENZ BOOKS

This edition is published by Lorenz Books

Lorenz Books is an imprint of Anness Publishing Ltd
Hermes House, 88–89 Blackfriars Road, London SE1 8HA
tel. 020 7401 2077; fax 020 7633 9499
www.lorenzbooks.com; info@anness.com

© Anness Publishing Ltd 2004

UK agent: The Manning Partnership Ltd, 6 The Old Dairy, Melcombe Road,
Bath BA2 3LR; tel. 01225 478444; fax 01225 478440; sales@manning-
partnership.co.uk

UK distributor: Grantham Book Services Ltd, Isaac Newton Way, Alma Park
Industrial Estate, Grantham, Lincs NG31 9SD; tel. 01476 541080; fax 01476 541061;
orders@gbs.tbs-ltd.co.uk

North American agent/distributor: National Book Network, 4501 Forbes
Boulevard, Suite 200, Lanham, MD 20706; tel. 301 459 3366; fax 301 429 5746;
www.nbnbooks.com

Australian agent/distributor: Pan Macmillan Australia, Level 18, St Martins
Tower, 31 Market St, Sydney, NSW 2000; tel. 1300 135 113; fax 1300 135 103;
customer.service@macmillan.com.au

New Zealand agent/distributor: David Bateman Ltd, 30 Tarndale Grove, Off
Bush Road, Albany, Auckland; tel. (09) 415 7664; fax (09) 415 8892

A CIP catalogue record for this book is available from the British Library.

Publisher: Joanna Lorenz
Editorial Director: Helen Sudell
Executive Editor: Joanne Rippin
Photographs: Michelle Garrett, Clare Park, Craig Knowles
Designers: Elizabeth Healey
Production Controller: Claire Rae

10 9 8 7 6 5 4 3 2 1

The author and publishers have made every effort to ensure that all
instructions contained within this book are accurate and safe, and
cannot accept liability for any resulting injury, damage or loss to
persons or property, however it may arise. If you do have any special
needs or problems, consult your doctor or a physiotherapist. This book
cannot replace medical consultation and should be used in conjunction
with professional advice.

contents

introduction

In today's technological age, there is increased pressure to work faster, play harder, and to do and have more of everything. It can seem like so many factors are beyond our control — added to personal pressures, there is the constant access to international news and information. Although this can be an exciting and stimulating lifestyle, it can also sometimes leave us feeling stressed or disorientated.

above
Burning incense can help you focus your meditation practice and lead you to a higher state of awareness.

opposite
Regular meditation calms body, mind and soul to improve your health and enhance the quality of your life.

However, there is a way to take charge of your life and to enhance and enrich its potential. Through regular meditation practice, you can find serenity within yourself, instead of having to rely on the outside world for your sense of security. Accepting responsibility for your own thoughts and feelings will, in turn, affect your health, your well-being and your transactions with others, and will have a positive effect on every aspect of your life.

In this book, we will look at techniques to help you reap the maximum benefits of meditation. Learning to still the body and quiet the mind are the first stepping stones to deeper consciousness. Breathing techniques will help you to find your own meditating rhythm; in addition, you will learn to focus by using sight, sound, smell and touch as triggers to more profound states of awareness.

We will also explore creative visualization, a technique to release past wounds and "rehearse" positive new situations, whether relating to relationships, career goals, spiritual understanding or improved physical health. Affirmations use the power of words to help you reach your goals.

Finally, there is a series of guided meditations to help you find calm and fulfilment. From contemplating your soul on the pathway of time, to meditating on what lies in your innermost heart, you will explore ways to expand your consciousness and transform your life. May you find peace and happiness.

meditation techniques

With the help of a few simple techniques, you can learn to meditate and enter into a wider, more

aware state of consciousness. Having achieved this peaceful state, where you are calm, focused

and loving, you can remember and use these attitudes at other times to enhance all

your daily interactions and relationships.

the need for mental peace

Underlying all meditation techniques is the impulse to quiet the mind, so that your thoughts become centred. From this position, you can reduce stress, put events and feelings into perspective and discover your changing self.

responding here and now

Most of us try to crowd too much into our lives, and so may lack the stillness and silence necessary to rebalance the nervous system. Regular meditation establishes a healthy rhythm of activity and rest for both mind and body. Our minds are constantly active, mulling over current problems, planning anxiously for a future we can't control, regretting past actions or creating personal plans, rules and opinions.

These mental "games" draw us, like magnets, away from the present moment. Meditation teaches us to live in the moment. When we wallow in negative emotions such as anger or resentment, meditation helps us to replace defensive energy-sapping reactions with open and trusting responses that enable us to build loving relationships.

reducing stress

Certain levels of stress are a normal part of life; a certain amount is essential for humans to be motivated and develop. However, the pace and complexity of modern life

far left
Stilling the mind through meditation gives the nervous system a much-needed rest from the stresses of everyday living.

left
Many of us have lives that are packed with activity from morning till night, leading to debilitating sensory overload.

can overburden the system and block our natural ability to manage pressure. We may become stuck in negative thought patterns, squandering our precious energy and unbalancing our ability to react appropriately to situations.

The human nervous system operates instinctively: it is programmed to deal physically with any threats to survival. Stress is a natural reaction that enables us to respond to danger, either by fighting or running away. Once the threatening episode is over, the nervous system should rebalance itself as we return to our normal level of activity; unfortunately, we may remain in a state of nervous over-stimulation, because we go on feeling anxious about past and future events.

rest and renewal

Because stress hormones make us feel excited, it is easy to become addicted to habits that trigger their release. This is why we watch exciting programmes on television and take part in challenging activities. But if we remain in a constant state of arousal, we deny our bodily systems the chance to rest and renew themselves. Stress accumulates until the system reaches breaking point – and the result is illness of the body or mind. By practising the techniques of meditation, we can reverse this build-up of stress by learning to consciously clear the mind and emotions of negative attitudes as we become aware of them.

above
Meditation can help to clear the mind and remind us that simple pursuits are often the most restorative and meaningful.

freeing vital energies

The chakras can be thought of as spinning wheels of energy sited up and down the body. Each correlates to a function of mind, body and soul. Meditation helps to clear and balance the chakras, allowing energy to flow in areas of our lives where it has become stagnant.

centres of energy

Stemming from key tenets of Hinduism and Tantric Buddhism, the chakras are focal points where psychic forces and functions of the body interact. Although there are said to be many thousands of chakras, the basic seven correlate to major nerve centres in the body. These relate not only to physical function but also to levels of consciousness, stages of life and spiritual development. The chakras are often described as lotus flowers, and meditation makes them bloom and perfume our lives with their positive attributes.

In healing techniques, the chakras are often represented by colours of the rainbow. When meditating, it is helpful to visualize the colour of the particular chakra on which you are focusing. In this way, you can help to free blocked-up energy and stimulate new energy in the areas of your life that need work.

seven basic chakras

life chakras:

1 Located at the base of the spine, the base chakra is concerned with survival and the sense of grounding to earth. When healthy, it is a deep, fiery red; it is dull, blackish red when unhealthy or stagnant.

left
The lotus flower is the symbol of the crown chakra, said to be our link between the human and the divine.

2 Found in the abdomen, lower back and sex organs, the sacral chakra is related to our role in human society, our emotions and our sexuality. When healthy, the sacral chakra is a glowing orange in colour, but is drab and brownish when lacking energy.

3 Located in the solar plexus, the navel chakra is related to personal power, self-esteem and metabolism. In its healthy state, it is a bright, sunny yellow; it may be tinged green when there is resentment or envy present.

love chakras:

4 The heart chakra is the middle of the system and is concerned with love, relationships, passion and deep feelings. Emerald green, or often its complementary colour, rose pink, when healthy it is faded when energy is blocked.

5 The throat chakra is related to communication, creativity and our experience of the world through vibration, such as in speaking or singing. It is a brilliant sapphire blue, especially when inspired or defending the truth.

light chakras:

6 Also known as the third eye, the brow chakra is related to intuition and seeing, both in a physical and a psychic sense. This is royal purple or amethyst, sometimes indigo.

7 At the top of the head, the crown chakra is related to consciousness and spiritual understanding; it is our link with the timeless universe. Brilliant white or pale lilac, it radiates like a beacon of light.

above
The seven chakras relate to the body, consciousness and spirituality.
1 - The base chakra
2 - The sacral chakra
3 - The navel chakra
4 - The heart chakra
5 - The throat chakra
6 - The brow chakra, or third eye
7 - The crown chakra

stilling the body

Before you begin to meditate, it is important to find a position that is comfortable for an extended period of time. Meditation is traditionally performed sitting with the back erect and vertical, so that energy flows smoothly up and down the spine and through the chakras.

When you are seated correctly, the brain and breathing function optimally and the chakras are balanced and full of vitality; an erect spine is easy to maintain if the right props are used. Regular practice is the best teacher, so that your body quickly adjusts to the new routine. When you find a comfortable position, practise sitting in it until you can remain motionless, relaxed yet alert, for half an hour or more. It is helpful to practise changing from one position to another without disturbing your inner focus.

sitting on a chair

When first beginning meditation practice, it may be easiest to sit upright on a firm chair or sofa. Your thighs should be parallel to the floor – you may need to raise your feet (without shoes) by resting them on a cushion. Sit erect with your hands together, palms upwards, resting on your thighs, with hands and feet parallel and pointing forwards. If you lean back, you will develop a backache, so sit erect with your spine straight. If this causes strain on your back, place some cushions behind you.

above left
You can meditate lying on the floor to induce a restful state without sleep.

far left
When first practising, you may find it easiest to sit upright in a chair.

left
With some practise, you may be able to maintain a cross-legged position, with each foot tucked under the opposite thigh.

lying down

You might feel more comfortable meditating lying down. If so, lie on your back, legs flat on the floor, feet slightly apart and relaxed. Position your arms away from the body, with your hands relaxed and open, palms facing upwards.

easy cross-legged pose

This position involves sitting erect, with the hips loose and knees wide. Each foot is tucked under the opposite thigh so that the weight of the legs rests on the feet rather than the knees. Place cushions under each thigh and/or under the buttocks if you feel pressure in the lower back. The tailbone (coccyx) should hang freely, letting the "sitting bones" take the weight of the trunk. Place your hands on your knees or rest them in your lap, with your palms facing up.

above
If you have time you might like to make meditation part of your bedtime or waking routine. Meditating in bed can be a good way to relax before sleep.

meditation in bed

Many people prefer to meditate first thing every morning, while the mind is still quiet from sleep, or use it as a technique to relax before going to sleep. If you meditate in bed, use a V-shaped pillow or ordinary pillows to support your back, so that you can sit erect in a cross-legged position. Drape a shawl around your shoulders so that you keep warm while you meditate. In the morning, choose a practice that energizes rather than relaxes you, such as chanting or repeating a mantra. You may prefer to keep your eyes open.

focusing the mind

To enjoy the full benefits of meditation, it helps to establish a regular time to practise, as well as a place in which you feel comfortable and secure. You may want to adorn this special corner with a few objects that will help you to relax and will also increase your concentration.

practice time

It is helpful to meditate at a regular time each day – when you wake up, before a meal or in the evening after a brisk walk, for example. You might read an uplifting book in bed and then meditate before going to sleep, or get up early before the household is awake. Whatever time you choose, stick to it to establish your meditation habit. Choose a time

when you are usually alone and undisturbed – the fuller your day, the more rewarding and de-stressing your meditation session can be.

quiet corner

Meditating in the same place will also help to establish your habit. Choose a quiet and uncluttered space, so that the moment you sit down, your mind becomes calm and focused. Make sure you are warm enough, as the body temperature drops when you relax and turn inwards. Your meditation corner might consist of a special chair in a peaceful part of your home, or perhaps a favourite cushion or a lovely rug. You might want to add a little table with a candle and some flowers, or anything you find soothing and inspiring to gaze at while you meditate.

opposite page
Creating a peaceful meditation corner with incense and candles encourages regular practice.

top right
Using the beautiful form of a fresh flower as a focus, you can guide your mind into the meditative state.

right
Staring into the flame of a single candle can help you to hone your focus in a technique called tratak.

objects of focus

The things you keep in your meditation corner can be used for the classic technique called tratak – or "gazing". This involves sitting erect and motionless while focusing your gaze upon an object. You can use a lighted candle as the point of focus – but check that there are no draughts to move the candle flame, as this can cause headaches. Epileptics and migraine sufferers should not gaze at a flame.

After gazing softly, without staring, close your eyes and keep the image in your mind's eye. When it fades, gaze at the candle again and repeat the visualization. Your mental image will gradually become firmer and your concentration deeper. Alternatively, a flower can be turned around in the hand, as you observe every detail of its beauty and structure. Holding a crystal, feeling its contours and coolness, is another form of tratak: here the "gazing" is accomplished through touch. Any object that inspires you can be used.

harnessing breathing

Regular breathing practice will calm the mind and raise your energy levels. A few rounds of breathing exercises through the day increases your lung capacity, preparing you for longer sessions during meditation.

Avoid any breathing practices after meals – when your stomach is full, it presses against your diaphragm, constricting your lungs. Keep your spine stretched and as straight as possible, whether you are standing, sitting, kneeling or lying down. This allows maximum lung expansion and helps the free flow of air and energy.

focus on the breathing muscles

This technique can be practised anywhere, sitting with the spine erect and the hands and eyes still. Place your hands on your knees, palms either up or down, with thumb and index fingers touching to close the energy circuits. As you breathe in deeply, feel your ribs expand and your diaphragm contract downwards against your stomach. Notice how these movements cause air to flow into your lungs.

As you breathe out, count "One and two and...", then stop your breath in mid-flow for the same count. Repeat until you have slowly and comfortably expelled enough air; repeat this cycle four times more then rest. Then reverse the cycle, breathing in and counting "One and two and..." and then out slowly for five breaths.

left
For maximum benefit, aim to keep your spine as erect as possible when practising breathing exercises.

opposite
Begin alternate nostril breathing by getting into meditation position and raising your hand towards your face.

alternate nostril breathing

This universally popular exercise quickly balances the nervous system, so that you feel calm and centred after just a few minutes. This breathing technique can be used either specifically to prepare you for meditation practice, or to refresh you during the course of the day.

Sit erect with your left hand on your knee or in your lap. Raise your right hand to place it against your face. Your thumb will close your right nostril, your index and middle fingers will rest against your forehead at the brow chakra and your ring finger will close your left nostril.

Your eyes may be closed, or open and gazing softly ahead. Keep your eyeballs still, as quiet eyes induce a quiet mind. Close your right nostril with your thumb. Breathe in through the left nostril.

Release the right nostril and close the left with your ring finger. Breathe out slowly, and then in again, through your right nostril. Then open the left nostril, close the right and breathe out. This is one round. Do five rounds, breathe naturally to rest, then repeat a few times.

above
Let your thumb close your right nostril, with index and middle fingers resting on the brow chakra, then take a breath.

above
Now let the ring finger close the left nostril and breath in through the right. Do five rounds of alternate breathing.

using the senses: sight and sound

Meditation techniques that help you to focus include turning your attention to an object or a particular sound. This helps to settle the mind and leads you through the portal of calming meditation. You can try several different focuses to find the method that works best for you.

inner sight

In the West, sight is probably our most conscious and developed sense. Our environment is constantly lit, and we are bombarded by visual messages, from traffic lights and billboards to television and computer screens. Many of us find it easier to picture something with the "mind's eye" than to feel or hear it, so visualization is a popular meditation technique.

Some colours are associated with relaxation and can be helpful to clear the mind of tension. Sit with your eyes closed, and be aware of the colour that comes into your mind. It may be any colour of the rainbow – red or purple, for example. Then slowly allow that colour to change to a blue, green or pink colour, allowing it to fill the whole of your mind's eye and replace all other colours. Your feeling of relaxation and inner peace will grow as the new colour builds in your mind.

tune your hearing

City noise pollution blunts our sense of hearing, yet this sense can take us more quickly and deeper into meditation than any of the others. An effective technique for

left
Experiment with different visual methods to lead your mind into the meditative state, whether staring into a flame or visualizing colours.

developing your listening ability is to sit quietly and focus upon your hearing. Start by identifying the most obvious sounds, such as a car in the street or a dog barking somewhere. Listen to these sounds, simply becoming aware of them without making any mental comment, such as "That is a dog's bark", or "That's ugly or loud." Gradually listen for more subtle sounds, such as your own breathing or heartbeat. Eventually, when you have learned how to listen impartially to sounds you are receiving, you will hear nada – your own inner vibration, which is sometimes likened to a high-pitched hum.

making your own sounds

Having learned to hear sounds impartially, you can start to produce your own sounds that are without any of the "mental baggage" that accompanies tuneful noises such as singing or playing musical instruments. You can chant a simple mantra, stroke a Tibetan singing bowl with a wooden wand, sing a scale or create rhythm on a drum – all without embarrassment or stress. Creating sounds is a wonderfully relaxing practice that can quickly take you into the meditative state.

above right
Focusing on the sound of bells is a gentle way to relax the mind and body so that deep meditation can occur.

right
When its rim is circled with a wooden wand, the Tibetan singing bowl emits a tone full of soothing natural harmonics.

using the senses: smell, taste, touch

Smell is our most basic sense and one that can recall instantly the memory of previous events, making it a useful trigger for meditation. Your tactile sense can also be used as an aid, either by touching an object or by focusing on the sensations of your physical body.

smell and taste

The senses of taste and smell are closely linked, each affecting the other extremely powerfully. They are our most primitive senses and the two lowest chakras, and they are essential for our survival. The most fleeting fragrances have the power to release emotions and memories, and in many religious traditions, aromatics such as incense are used to elevate the spirit or to induce altered states of consciousness.

Smell can be included in your meditation by burning incense or fragrant oils. Your taste buds can also assist the practice: you can make eating or drinking – savouring slow mouthfuls – a potent exercise in awareness.

far left
The sense of taste can be used to hone your attention; for example, slowly savour the tang of fresh lemon.

above left
The ancient practice of using worry beads employs the sense of touch in a repetitive way, aiding concentration.

below left
Many people burn incense to focus the mind – pungent aromas can release long-forgotten emotions and memories.

opposite
You can experiment with, and alternate between, different kinds of sensation to harness your awareness.

exploring touch

Every emotional response is a matter of "feeling" that involves some aspect of the physical sense of touch. Feeling safe is like being held by loving hands or feeling the presence of friends around you. Feeling inspired or uplifted creates a tangible feeling of inner lightness and expansion. You can also feel "in touch" with your body – whether you are hot or cold, comfortable or in pain, still or moving.

Most of these sensations remain below consciousness unless we need to notice them. In our daily lives, we are unaware of the muscles that keep us standing upright until a time when we trip or are in danger of falling, or of our breathing cycles until we run too fast and become out of breath. Learning consciously to feel safe and relaxed while becoming more focused and aware is a wonderful antidote to stress.

You can use your sense of touch in a lulling, soothing way to induce a state of meditation. Children often do this by rubbing a corner of a blanket or satin ribbon against their fingers when they feel tense or insecure; both adults and children may be seen absent mindedly curling a lock of hair around their finger. The same technique is seen all over the Middle East, where worry beads are rhythmically passed through the fingers to focus the mind and calm anxiety. In a similar way, you can hold one or two smooth stones for your meditation, passing them slowly from hand to hand.

creative
imagining

Research has shown that the mind perceives vividly imagined experiences as though they are really happening to us in the present. During the relaxed state of meditation — when we are calm, aware, focused, happy and loving — we can use visualization to let go of past wounds and rehearse future successes.

the art of creative visualization

Simply put, visualization is a form of focused daydreaming that helps to programme your unconscious mind to help you achieve changes in your life. With a few guidelines, you can create scenes that alter your way of thinking, feeling and being, and thus transform your life.

below
You can close your eyes anywhere and rehearse a forthcoming event in your life.

creative imagining

It is said that we always get more of what we focus on, so it makes great sense to focus on what we want: a positive, healthy and happy life, rich in loving relationships, satisfying work and rewarding pursuits. Visualization is a technique that brings the senses into full play to enable us to imagine changes needed to build up this happy inner world, which will then be reflected in the outer world. This type of relaxed imagining is used in many different types of therapies, because it can help us to change our perceptions

and the way in which others treat us by changing the way we feel inside ourselves.

As well as practicing when sitting in an upright meditation pose, visualization can be done lying down or reclining. This means that we can help ourselves to feel better when we are tired or depleted, ill in bed, or simply want to enter into a peaceful state so that we sleep well.

close your eyes and breathe

After bringing your body and mind into a calm state, imagine yourself in a situation, behaving, acting and looking as you would wish to do. Perhaps you want to prepare for a job interview or to ask someone on a date; perhaps you are rehearsing a performance or preparing for a competition.

Imagine being there in as much detail as possible: feeling the atmosphere, seeing the colours, hearing the sounds, smelling the scents. Imagine what the outcome will mean for you, then explore your reactions, and feel the warm, happy feelings of your success. If any negative thoughts invade your mind, push them away and replace them with positive ones. The more your mind rehearses a positive outcome, the more likely is your chance of success.

above right
Early morning, when the mind has just emerged from the dreaming state, is a good time for creative visualization.

right
Visualizing an important conversation in a relaxed state beforehand can help you to achieve a positive outcome.

affirmations

You can use affirmations — short, positive statements — for your long-term benefit. By using affirmations in combination with visualization exercises, and repeating them at other times of the day, it is possible to make lasting changes in your life.

above
You can empower your mind by guiding it into a more positive state using affirmations.

the power of words

The first step is to decide on an affirmation and repeat it when you are in a state of deep relaxation: what positive changes in your behaviour, perception or attitude would make you more like the person you wish to be? You can then visualize a scene that activates all five senses, so that you become fully present in a place where you feel naturally safe and relaxed. Once this scene is set, you can go deeper and reinforce the changes you've chosen. The unconscious mind is happy to respond to suggestions put to it by the conscious mind — provided that your nervous system is in a thoroughly relaxed state, and that you express your intention correctly.

- Phrase your affirmation clearly, mentioning just one change at a time.
- Describe it in the present tense, such as "I am... [happy, healthy, confident, successful at... or forgiving of...]" The unconscious mind lives only in the present and ignores the past and future.
- Express your affirmation in positive terms only.
- Repeat your affirmation three times, slowly, so that your unconscious mind knows you mean business. In this way, you are programming it to carry out your intentions — even when the conscious mind is busy with other things.

below

Affirmations are more effective when repeated daily. Set aside a regular time when you can relax for 10 minutes.

right

Choose affirmations that reflect your goals, for example: "I enjoying cooking and am very creative with food."

key affirmations

for creativity:

- *I love to express myself in creative ways.*
- *I enjoy my own imaginative responses to the world.*

for living in the present:

- *I have learned a great deal from the past.*
- *The future is an exciting range of opportunities.*
- *I am able to enjoy my acute awareness of this moment.*
- *I am laying good foundations NOW on which to build a better future.*

for goal achievement:

- *Step by step, I am moving in the right direction.*
- *I have the ability and determination to achieve my goals.*
- *With the right attitude I can achieve my ambitions.*

for reducing stress:

- *I enjoy solving problems and work well under pressure.*
- *I am a calm, methodical and efficient worker.*
- *I love the feeling of having achieved so much in a day.*
- *I can sort out my priorities and direct my energies appropriately.*

the beach scene

The beauty, warmth and peace of a tropical beach make it pleasing to all the senses, so it is an ideal subject for a visualization to help you create your happy inner world. The more detail you add, the more complete your experience will be.

This visualization can help you to change a behaviour or aspect of your life that needs adjusting. Decide what your resolve is before you begin. First, allow your body to enter a state of deep relaxation by doing some stretching and deep breathing exercises. Sit or lie down in a comfortable position and start to imagine yourself reclining on a beautiful beach. Now, lying back on soft sand near the water's edge on this pleasant sunny day, use all your senses to appreciate every detail of the scene, so that you experience it fully. Feel the gritty texture and

dampness of the sand beneath you, dig your toes into it and let it run through your fingers. Look at the scenery around you, the deep blue of the sea and sky, the pale sand, the distant horizon, a few fluffy white clouds, seagulls flying overhead. You can hear the seagulls calling, waves lapping across the sand and the sound of a gentle breeze moving the leaves of the trees behind you. You can smell the salt air and taste it on your lips . What else can you feel, see and hear? Perhaps the air caressing your body, the intricate patterns of individual grains of sand, the soft pastel colours and exquisite shapes of tiny shells, the sound of children laughing in the distance. When you have built up the details of this lovely scene, stay in it for a while, enjoying feelings of peace and contentment, gratefulness and relaxation. The purpose of this visualization is to bring you to this inner place where you know that "all is well". Before you leave the beach repeat the resolve you have decided on, slowly and clearly three times. Then gradually let the scene dissolve, knowing it is always there for you to return to at any time, no matter what is going on in the external world.

chakra fields

This visualization takes you on a journey that starts with your everyday awareness and leads to a higher level of consciousness. In it, you will imagine walking slowly through the countryside and up a hill to your goal, before returning by the same route.

Start by walking along a lane that leads to a field with a sea of red flowers – their vivid red represents the vitality and growth of the base chakra. Follow a footpath up the hill, where a gate takes you into a grove of orange trees laden with ripe fruit, representing the sensuality of the sacral chakra. Eat some delicious fruit, then enter a field of golden sunflowers, representing the light and heat of the navel chakra, where reserves of energy are kept – just as sunflower seeds store the energy of life. Feast your eyes on the gold around you, and let your skin soak up

the warmth from the sun. As you continue, you see another gate leading to a walled garden with a long archway festooned with pink climbing roses exuding heavenly scents. This represents your heart chakra, with its atmosphere of peace and joy. Touch the velvety petals and take a bloom to keep. Through another gate and find yourself on high ground under a wide blue sky; birds are flying and calling to each other. The sky is reflected in pools of blue water from melting snows. This scene represents the throat chakra and the energies of pure space and sound. Someone calls your name and you walk towards a high pass ahead of you. He or she comes to meet you, offering to guide you; this represents your own higher wisdom, found in the brow chakra, source of insight. Your guide leads you over the pass. Beyond is a grassy glade surrounded by trees. In the centre is a small white building – a special, spiritual place – that represents your crown chakra. Your guide gestures to you to enter. There you sit and repeat your resolve, slowly and clearly, three times. When you feel it is time to return, walk slowly back the way you have come, knowing that you can return whenever you wish.

the pathway of time

Although we cannot change the past, we can learn from it, building up skills and useful insights from what we have experienced along the way. Now is the only moment in which we can truly make an impact, and future goals provide a sense of direction.

Imagine standing on a pathway that stretches in front of you and trails behind you, the way you have come. As you look round, you are aware that the area around you — to the left, right and above — is brilliantly illuminated, and that sounds are amazingly clear. You are intensely aware of all that is happening around you, and your reactions to it. Look ahead again: you see the path in front, but it is dim in comparison with the area. As you check over your shoulder, notice that the path behind is even less clear. A distant clock chimes and you take a step forward with

an acute awareness, you notice the slightest of noises and shifts of light and take

pleasure even in the sound of silence. You hear the same clock ticking, and with

each tick take a small step forwards, effortlessly, along the path…illumination and

awareness move with you in the here and now. At any fork in the path, you make

decisions easily and quickly, as you are truly involved in the moment. You enjoy

an acute awareness of sound, feeling, taste and smell. Further along the path, you

focus your attention on a goal: personal, career, social or spiritual. Imagine

yourself in a situation where you have achieved this goal, surrounded by the things

or people that show your achievement. Be as specific as you can, and aware of all

you see, hear, touch or sense, and think about how achieving this goal makes you

feel, how it affects your mood and your feelings about yourself. Now, from where

you are at that moment of achieving that goal look back down the pathway of

time to where you were, and notice the stages of movement towards achieving the

goal. Feel more and more determined to make one change at a time, to achieve

your goal, and to take the first step towards it today.

the peaceful retreat

Imagine that you are visiting a beautiful old country house in a quiet, remote area, on a warm summer's afternoon. As you meditate, try to drink in all the details, the atmosphere and the history of the place, and visualize life here through the centuries.

Begin by standing at the top of the wide, ceremonial staircase that leads down to the entrance hall. There is no one around to bother you… You slowly begin to ease down the steps… now you are moving down the last ten steps to the hallway, relaxing more as each foot reaches the next step: 10 Taking one step down, relax and let go… 9 Take the next step down, feel at ease… 8 Becoming more relaxed, let go even more… 7 Drift deeper… and deeper… and even deeper down still …

6 Become calmer… and calmer…even calmer still… 5 Continue to relax…

4 Relaxing even more , let go… 3 Sinking deeper, drifting even further into this

welcoming, relaxed state… 2 Enjoy these good feelings, feelings of inner peace…

1 Nearly all the way down, feeling beautifully relaxed, you reach 0.

Now you wander towards the open doors and gardens, soaking up the atmosphere

of peace and permanence in this lovely old building. You wander out through the

doors and find yourself standing on a wide gravel drive that leads to the lush green

lawns, and the shrubs and trees, different shades of green and brown against a

clear, blue sky. There are flowerbeds with splashes of colour bobbing in the gentle

breeze, and there's no one else about, no one needing anything or expecting

anything from you, you can enjoy the serenity and solitude of this pleasant garden

that has existed for centuries. You notice a pond, and wander towards it, the gravel

crunching beneath your feet. At the edge of the pond you look down into the

clear, cool water, gazing at the fish of red and gold, black and silver, swimming

effortlessly in and out of shadows and around the lily pads, their scales catching

the sunlight. As you watch the fish, your mind becomes even more deeply relaxed.

the sphere of protection

Visualizing a protective bubble around you can help you to feel more in control. It can change your whole response to the many challenging demands of modern living, and at the same time improve your confidence in yourself, your work and relationships.

Imagine yourself in a situation that has caused stress in the past. Picture the situation, and the other people involved. See yourself there, and notice a slight shimmer of light between yourself and those other people , a sort of bubble around you… a protective bubble that reflects any negative feelings back to them, leaving you able to get on with the tasks in your life with an inner strength and calmness that surprises you. A protective, invisible bubble surrounds you at all

times. It only allows feelings that are positive and helpful to you to pass through for you to enjoy and build upon. Stress and negativity can be infectious, but you are protected, you keep things in perspective and deal with things calmly and methodically. You are able to see the way forward and solve problems by using your own inner resources and strengths. See yourself talking to someone who has been causing tension in your life. Tell them that what they are doing is unhelpful in resolving the problem or difficulty, and let them know in a very calm way that they can accept it without offence. See yourself being able to supply examples and information until they understand your position. At all times, you are surrounded by that protective bubble of light that keeps you calm and quietly confident. Next, imagine pushing out through the bubble emotions that are unhelpful… past resentments, hurts and embarrassments. Push them to where they can no longer limit or harm you. The bubble stays with you and enables you to remain in control, keeping things in perspective with the strength to change those things you can change, accept those things that you cannot, and move on.

the haven

This visualization can help you rediscover the magic that exists at the source of your life.

Once you've reached a relaxed state, close your eyes and allow your mind to drift to a place

— real or imaginary — that is special, a place where you feel good about yourself.

Where is this special corner of the world? It may be a meadow you visited as a

child, in a quiet part of a wood, or a secret room in a ruined castle, where you

found yourself suddenly away from other people. Perhaps it is a windswept beach,

where pieces of driftwood wash up on the sand… or a cave you came upon when

the tide was out. Go to the place and explore it… feel what made it special… what

makes it special still… it belongs only to you, so you can think and do whatever you like here… In this safe, secure place, no one and nothing can ever bother you. Allow yourself to realize that this is a haven, a unique haven of tranquillity, where you will always feel able to relax completely… Now you can allow your mind to drift… Notice what sort of light shines in through the branches or the window or the drifting clouds… Is it bright or hazy?… Does the temperature feel soothingly warm or refreshingly cool? Be aware of the colours that surround you… the outlines of shapes… the textures. What sounds do you hear? Distant voices or perhaps birds singing… ocean waves lapping against the shore or the chiming of ancient church bells… Be aware of the colours, shapes and textures that surround you, the familiar objects that make that place special. You can just be there, sitting, lying or reclining, enjoying the sounds, smells, and atmosphere. No one is asking anything of you here, no one expects anything of you, you don't need to be anywhere except here, where everything is peaceful and you can truly relax.

Breathe in the quiet solitude and feel at one with your private place.

meditations
of peace

During an experience of meditation, we are able to release cares, worries and

attachments, allowing calm to suffuse the emotions and an overactive nervous system.

When we enter into this place of peace, we are enhancing the quality of our lives,

healing our bodies and enriching our souls.

working with your feelings

Feelings can rule our lives if we let them — we may allow love and excitement, as well as pain and dissatisfaction, overwhelm us. By exploring sensations caused by feelings, we can come to understand their purpose in our lives and so learn crucial lessons from them.

good and bad feelings

True peace and transcendence depend upon cultivating and maintaining good feelings and a positive outlook on life. Gratitude, acceptance, respect and personal responsibility are some of the positive qualities that make us feel good. Reflecting on these qualities brings peace and joy, helping to lead us inwards towards a state of deep meditation.

When we are lonely or isolated, embarrassed or angry, we feel bad in the life chakras, and we experience good feelings when socializing happily or moving toward a goal. Negative feelings can arise in the love chakras from self-centredness or blocked self-expression, and positive feelings come through sharing. In the light chakras, positive feelings come with understanding and access to higher wisdom, whereas negative feelings result from confusion and a sense of disjointedness. If we understand that every negative feeling has a positive intent behind it, we are on the way to achieving greater happiness and fulfilment.

working with opposites

The following technique, based on experiencing "opposites", allows you to become impartially aware of your feelings, many of which may be below consciousness:

- Relax deeply – sitting, reclining or lying on your back.
- Imagine various "pairs of opposites" and notice the physical sensations that arise.
- Start with pairs that have little or no positive/negative emotional associations – such as hot/cold, hard/soft,

light/dark – and observe how your body feels.

- Move on to a more emotionally challenging pair, starting with the positive side, and observe what feelings are evoked: birth/death, spacious/confined, happy/sad and delighted/angry are some examples.
- Observe what feelings arise in your body as you contemplate the negative half of the pair – so that you can identify them from now on and understand what "pushes your buttons". You can then take the appropriate action to make you feel better and defuse tension in and around you.
- Repeat the positive half of the pair before moving on to the next pair of opposites.
- End with some gentle, deep breathing before coming out of relaxation.

left
Feelings can point to important life lessons; exploring them can help us to understand ourselves and others.

above right
Focusing on the feelings aroused by a colour, such as red, can help to unlock stifled desires and frustrations.

stillness, silence and sensitivity

Simple steps can help you focus your attention, and bring stillness to your body and mind. In this way, you will pave an easier path into the meditative state, so that you can enjoy the full benefits of deep contemplation.

above
Achieving stillness can be facilitated by finding a quiet spot where you can meditate undisturbed.

the three s's

Stillness is the first step towards meditation. If you sit relaxed and completely still, you'll help your mind to drift into a poised state of awareness where inner material can begin to flow. Next comes silence: many people try to use music to blot out sounds in the environment, but it is much better to find a quiet time of day and learn to create inner silence. This matters because, as well as seeing images, you may hear sounds. Sensitivity is the third skill you need to use: listen, watch and perceive whatever images, sounds, symbols or other sensations occur in your mind. These may be vague at first, but the more still you are, the sharper your awareness will become.

the seagull: soaring towards freedom

The following movements will help you to free yourself from distractions and focus upon the heart chakra, where you can embrace uplifting states, accept and balance emotions and heal past traumas. They can also help you to forgive others and yourself, letting go of all the hurt, anger and resentment, allowing yourself the freedom to move forwards in your life. The seagull lives totally in the present moment, visualize yourself flying high in the blue sky and let all negativity go, releasing it as you breathe out and filling the space in your heart with fresh glory on each in-breath.

1 Kneel on a mat, with a cushion or bolster between your legs. Sit on the cushion and bring your palms together at the heart chakra.

2 As you breathe out, bend forwards and place your forehead on the floor, keeping your hands and elbows as high as possible and stretching your chest. Surrender and empty your lungs.

3 As you breathe in, sit up, lift your sternum and stretch your arms like wings wide to the sides. Look up and joyfully surrender to the air, the moment and the movement. Surrender and fill your lungs. Repeat for several minutes.

chanting from within

By giving your attention to a simple repetitive chant you will become aware of every detail of what you are doing, and enter into the moment. In this state of awareness, the mind witnesses without judgement or reaction.

verbal mantras

OM, or AUM, is recognized in many cultures as the primordial sound, whose vibration brought the universe into being. Repetition of the OM mantra on a daily basis, chanted aloud, whispered or repeated silently, is said to have a cumulative and profoundly beneficial effect. When chanted aloud, the OM sound – pronounced as in "home" – should be deep and full, with the vibrations resonating in the life chakras, then moving up into the chest, where the love chakras are sited, and finally closing with a long, humming "mmm" in the head and the light chakras – all on one deep, steady, continuous note.

The syllable can also be divided into three sounds: A is the beginning of life, time and forms; U is maintained through the relationships of cosmic love; and M comes when we experience personally that all is spirit – and the rest is mental illusion.

far left
Prepare to chant your verbal mantra by making your meditation place light, comfortable and conducive to concentration.

left
The "OM" or "AUM" mantra uses three primordial sounds that deeply effect body and mind, unifying them in one steady note.

written mantras

Likhit japa is the traditional practice of writing or drawing a mantra over and over again, rather than chanting it aloud. The mantra most often used in this form of meditation is OM, which is carefully drawn numerous times on a page while you repeat the sound silently in your mind each time. Like other repetitive tasks, likhit japa is a way to keep the mind focused and still.

You can write mantras in many different ways. For example, you may want to keep a notebook and a pencil in your pocket and simply draw neat rows of OMs across the page whenever you have a spare moment, perhaps aiming for a definite number on each page.

Other mantras can be copied out in a similar way, or you can use a phrase that is meaningful to you, such as "world peace". Repeat this with intent in your thought vibrations: every action starts with a thought, and if enough people think the same thought, they can change the world. Alternatively, you may wish to draw a symbol, such as a dove, to represent your repeated phrase, covering your page with a flock of birds that will continue to remind you of the thought you sent out to the world.

life-light-love mantra

Repeating this mantra, taken from the Isha Upanishad, will help you to glimpse the truth of divine life-light-love and absolute unity:

That eternal life-light-love is full; this changing world is full.
From full, the full is taken; the full has come.
If you take out full from the full, the full alone remains.

above
You may wish to create your own written or drawn mantra, or you can simply pencil a row of OMs over and over.

vibrating with the universe

It is said that the universe began with a sound – OM, the primordial syllable – and every atom vibrates at its own frequency. We can tune into our own place in the system by learning to recognize our unique internal sounds, or nada.

above
By focusing on nada, your own internal sound, you can harness greater awareness of and from the universe.

nada

Each of us can become aware of our own personal vibratory note when we insulate the senses from distraction during meditation and turn all our attention inwards. This sound - called nada – is often heard at first as a high-pitched, vibrational hum, such as you might hear when standing beneath overhead power cables. It is often described as having several levels of subtlety, from the sounds of the ocean, a kettledrum or gong, to the gentler sounds of bells tinkling or bees humming.

Focusing on nada calms the mind and brings greater spiritual and physical awareness to our lives. Anyone who has learned to relax, still the chattering mind and really listen will be able to hear nada.

chanting through the chakras

This powerful practice, which involves chanting a musical scale through the chakras, can help you to perceive and recognize nada, the inner vibration or sounds.

Chant OM in each chakra, drumming to accompany the chanting if you wish. Start with any comfortably low note and ascend a scale to finish an octave higher. The key of C major is often used, chanting C for the base chakra, D for the sacral chakra and so on. After A for the brow chakra, you'll need another chakra on which to chant B, so focus upon bindu – the point at the back of the head where

Buddhist monks sometimes wear a tuft of hair. The crown chakra then becomes C, an octave above the base chakra. This octave represents the "human" realm.

1 The octave above the crown chakra represents the "divine" realm, and the one below the base chakra is the "animal" (or subhuman) realm. We have chakras in all three realms, and many more – and each of these will resonate as you chant.

2 Ascend and descend through the chakras three times before pausing in silence to feel the effects, take your energy down into your feet to ground yourself.

chanting in a group

A meditation that chants through the chakras is particularly effective when done in a group. Each person sounds his or her own note, all taking a breath in together when indicated by the leader, and then chanting A, U or M on the slow breath out. The meditation ends with everyone chanting OM on their own note and in their own rhythm, so that the sounds mingle together until a natural pause occurs. Silence follows until the meditation ends with a grounding exercise. The more people that join in the OM chanting, the more powerful the effects become, and the longer the subsequent silence is likely to continue.

top
Playing percussion instruments in a group is a way to "feel" each other's rhythms as a prelude to chanting.

above
Chanting through the chakras in a group can be a profound method of connecting with others.

waterlily meditation

Meditating on the growth of a water lily will help you to understand the concept of the "great chain of being", and to find your own vibratory note within it. The chain concept forms the basis of the mystical Kabbala in the West and the chakra system in the East.

Human beings are the link between the vibrationally lower and higher states of being, with no one state being better or worse than another. The evolutionary path naturally leads up to greater complexity and higher consciousness, but however high we may rise, we remain firmly attached to the point where we began: rather than moving, we have expanded our entire being. The growth of the lotus or water lily illustrates the spanning of different "realms" or states. Some ideas for meditation on this subject are suggested here. You can concentrate on

one or all of the lily's stages, but your own intuition can add many other insights:

The solid state (life): The plant begins at the bottom of the lake, with a tiny root delving into the solid mud from where it draws its nourishment for life. The mud is heavy, sticky, and uncompromising – yet full of nutrients that are essential to survival. It also provides a firm foundation and anchors the plant. This stage corresponds to our physical state that anchors us in our current incarnation.

The liquid state (light): The tiny plant grows a stem and slowly rises up through the water, towards the shimmering light. Water represents the flow of our emotions and thoughts. Just as their permeability to light helps shoots grow into leaves and buds, so our experiences expand our sensitivity and awareness.

The gaseous state (love): Eventually the leaves and buds of the water lily reach the surface and are exposed to the warmth of the air above the water. Here the flower opens under the touch of the sun and blissfully surrenders its beauty and perfume. It is fertilized with pollen so that the new seeds grow and drop into the mud at the bottom of the lake to start the cycle once more.

meditation for inner clarity

A period of meditation provides the time and space you need to keep your inner world

"clean" — free from the incessant dialogue of worries, anxieties and fears. This meditation

will help you to create the space for spiritual harmony, which will filter down to mind and

body, and subtly infuse your surroundings with balanced and peaceful vibrations. You will

feel revitalized physically, your mind will be refreshed and your emotions calmed.

Practise this simple meditation to help keep you, your home and your workplace

free from stress. Set an alarm clock to ring after ten minutes, and place it beside

you. Sit comfortably on a straight-backed chair with your feet flat on the floor.

Imagine that your spine is being slowly stretched upwards towards the heavens and down towards the earth, and that the central point of balance is in your abdomen. Breathe fully, slowly, concentrating only on your breathing. Breathe in the word "peace" and allow it to infuse your whole breathing. Breathe out the phrase "freedom from fear". At first your thoughts may race, your concentration may wander and you may feel restless. Continue to breathe and bring your mind back to the words on rising and falling breaths. You will feel a sense of calm as you maintain your focus. Sit in contemplation until the alarm rings. On an out breath, open your eyes, and as you do so imagine the sunrise coming out of them.

cave of the heart

Our cave of the heart is a sacred haven, untouched by any negativity or doubt. It is a place where we can feel safe, supported and healed. The following meditation will help you to discover this, so that you can go there whenever you need help or comfort.

Imagine you are in a luminous bubble that is suspended in space between heaven and earth. This sphere is your aura. A silvery cord attaches it firmly to heaven, then passes through your body seated in the centre of your aura and attaches it firmly to the earth. Now look within your aura. The silver cord that passes through your body has your chakras strung along it like beads on a necklace. Imagine yourself breathing deeply, seated inside your aura. As you breathe in you

are drawing light down from the heavenly end of the cord, and life up from the earthly end. As you breathe out, puff this mixture into your aura, as though into a balloon, so that it gets brighter and bigger. Continue pumping both light (consciousness) and life (vitality) into your aura until it feels radiant and healthy. See yourself sitting in your "mind space", which is like a room with a front wall of mirrored glass. You can look through it to see the external world, but it also reflects back your own thoughts and mental pictures. Now imagine yourself standing up to leave your "mind space" and going down a staircase, to the level of your "heart space". On this level is a door. Open it and walk into the "cave of your heart", where you see a low table, upon which a small lamp is burning – the eternal divine flame, the symbol of who you really are. Around the table are benches. Sit down and gaze into the flame, letting its warmth and joy permeate and heal you at every level. When you are ready, let the scene dissolve and give it to the earth by breathing out deeply. Come out of meditation slowly. Repeat this meditation until, you can rest in its healing presence at any time.

using a mandala in meditation

A graphic symbol of the universe, the mandala can be used as a focus to enhance and deepen your meditation and help you to solve a problem or decide which path to take. You can use a traditional Buddhist or Hindu mandala or make one for yourself.

focusing the mind

By giving all your attention to a simple repetitive task, you become aware of every detail of what you are doing. In this relaxed state of awareness, the mind simply witnesses what is happening without judging or reacting to it. The mind, therefore, stays clear, attentive and receptive. A good way to achieve this state is to use a mandala, either one that you feel drawn to or one that you have created yourself.

mandala gazing

Before you prepare yourself and the room for meditation, consider any issues that have been troubling you and select a mandala that you feel will help you to resolve those problems. To create a soporific atmosphere, light candles and incense, play soft and soothing music, and make sure you have a comfortable place to sit.

left
Before gazing at the mandala, do gentle breathing exercises and focus on solving your problems.

right
Create the right atmosphere for meditating on your mandala with fresh flowers and mellow music.

1 Close your eyes for a few minutes and take some deep breaths. Aim to become still and silent in yourself so that you are ready to explore all the depth and subtlety of the mandala's intricate design.

2 Now open your eyes and gaze at the mandala. Notice which parts of it attract you, and explore its shapes, patterns and colours with your eyes. See what is on the edge and what is in the centre of the design.

3 You may find that defocusing your eyes slightly will help you to see more deeply into the mandala and allow it to "speak" to you. Sit and gaze at it, letting thoughts triggered by the mandala rise and fall, all the time remaining focused on the image. Spend at least five minutes concentrating on this meditation.

4 Once you feel you have drunk in all the details, close your eyes and remember for a moment the parts of the mandala that held the strongest attraction for you. What did those patterns mean to you? Did they have any particular messages for you about your life? If so, how can you use what you've learned to make changes in your life?

5 When you open your eyes, have in mind one action that you will do in response to listening to your inner voice.

above
Drawing or colouring in your own mandala can have a refreshingly therapeutic effect.

right
Once you've finished working on the mandala, drink in its patterns and contemplate what they mean to you.

meeting your own soul

It is through meditation that we truly experience our "soul level": we learn to listen to our own souls, and to reach out to other souls and the world around us. In this visualization, you can discover your "heart home", a place where only love exists, for yourself and for others.

In this meditation, visualize yourself wearing robes of shimmering energies that both symbolize and veil the brightness of the spirit. Settle into a still and peaceful state, ready to visualize. See yourself wrapped in your protective aura, which is firmly attached by a silver cord to the heaven (light) and earth (life) poles and suspended between them. This cord passes through your chakras within your aura. Breathe in both light (from above) and life (from below) at the same time, so that they mingle as love. Breathe this out into your aura. See yourself leaving your

"mind space" and walking down into the area of your "heart space". Settle in front of the eternal flame that burns in a tiny lamp on a low table at the centre of your heart home. Gaze into this flame of love and enter a state of peace. After a while, look around your heart home and notice how it contains objects or images that remind you of those, alive or dead, with whom you share a bond. Love's bonds are eternal. Take comfort and support from this understanding. Look down at your soul robes of swirling energy. What colours do you see? They are your personal "energy signature". Look around you — your heart home will become adorned, as your loving relationships leave their impressions behind in the form of beautiful images. Let the images dissolve before grounding yourself. Alternatively, before finishing, you may wish to invite another soul to share your space. They will appear quietly on a seat beside you. True souls are always in a state of peace. The ongoing healing effects upon both personalities can be truly amazing. Enjoy this meeting, thank them for responding and allow their image to dissolve before coming out of the meditation.

group meditation

Each of us feels the need for help with healing at certain times, whether of old or new

wounds, physical, emotional, mental or spiritual. With this meditation you can generate

positive energy and love to help you move forward. A group mediation is a powerful

expression of universal oneness, uniting all the members in living cooperation and faith. The

meditation may be directed towards a specific goal, such as world peace, or a healing.

Your group should sit in a circle facing a candle in the centre – this represents the

person or group in need of healing, or the whole planet and all living beings.

Allow the group some time to get settled, and nominate someone to lead the

session. When everyone is ready, the nominated person should light the candle to

begin. Each person then concentrates on connecting with above (representing light) and below (representing life) and, on each breath in, draws light down and life up simultaneously into the group aura. Imagine the group aura like a huge balloon that encompasses the whole group keeping the candle flame at its centre. On each breath out, this group aura becomes filled with love energy, and grows ever brighter. Continue this section of the meditation for a few minutes, strengthening the group aura. When the nominated person feels it is time to move to the next stage, direct the breathing in of light and life and the breathing out of love, specifically into the flame of the candle at the centre of the group, while visualizing total healing. Continue to direct healing energy towards the centre of the group for a few minutes. Let the images slowly dissolve, breathe deeply and take your energy down into your feet to ground yourself, before opening your eyes. Give thanks for the healing received and channelled by each member of the group, and then extinguish the candle flame to end the meditation.

index